Empath's Ultimate Guide To Shield Yourself From Negative Energies

Simple Action Plan Included

SANDY QUINN

(AKA
Empath's 5-Minute Action Plan To Shield Yourself From Negative Energies Now)

Introduction

Are you tired of being constantly drained by negative people and events around you? To make matters worse, do you often feel afraid to say "no" to family, friends and colleagues asking for help? At the end of the day, do you collapse onto your bed exhausted emotionally and physically but unable to fall asleep because you were still affected by the events of the day?

In this book, you will discover what lies at the root of your problems and why you unknowingly attract negative people and energies into your life. You will discover a simple action plan to shield yourself effectively - no longer spending all your precious time and energy to serve other people's expectations.

For most of my life, I was an overachiever from school to sports but also a "Yes-er" to everyone until I became a burnout. What I realized from my experience and that of others is that it is a fine line that separates those of us who are struggling empaths from those who are empowered empaths.

Whatever struggles you are experiencing as an empath, you will benefit from the simple but effective strategies which have allowed me and others to break free from negative energies and reclaim our birthrights. This book offers you a simple action plan - which, like a map, will lead you without fail to your best life ever.

Don't live your life being affected by other people's negative energies. Be the sort of person who dare to step out to take action without hesitation. Let others be amazed by your transformation such that they know you're no longer a "Yes-er".

After going through this book you will begin to feel more confident as you start freeing yourself from negative energies. The best part is you can now finally focus on yourself and what's truly important to you. Live the best life you can imagine now.

Scroll up to the top and Click Buy Now.

Table of Contents

Introduction — 3

Chapter 1: My Story — 7

Chapter 2: Am I An Empath? — 9

Chapter 3: My Gifts As An Empath — 11

Chapter 4: Is An Empath and Being Empathic the Same Thing? — 13

Chapter 5: Am I Also A Highly Sensitive Person (HSP)? — 15

Chapter 6: Your Outlook In Life As An Empath — 17

Chapter 7: Why Do I Attract Energy Vampires? (And How To Get Rid Of Them) — 19

Chapter 8: 7 Simple Strategies You Can Use In 5-Minute To Shield Yourself — 25

Chapter 9: Embracing Your Gifts — 37

Chapter 10: Empath's Quick Guide to Living — 43

Epilogue — 47

Check Out My Other Book — 48

Text Copyright © 2017 Sandy Quinn

All rights reserved. No part of this guide may be reproduced in any form without permission in writing from the publisher except in the case of brief quotations embodied in critical articles or reviews.

Legal & Disclaimer

The information contained in this book and its contents is not designed to replace nor take the place of any form of medical or professional advice; it is not meant to replace the need for independent medical, financial, legal or other professional advice or services, as may be required. The content and information in this book has been provided for educational and entertainment purposes only.

The content and information contained in this book has been compiled from sources deemed reliable, and it is accurate to the best of the Author's knowledge, information and belief. However, the Author cannot guarantee its accuracy and validity and cannot be held liable for any errors and/or omissions. Further, changes are periodically made to this book as and when needed. Where appropriate and/or necessary, you must consult a professional (including but not limited to your doctor, attorney, financial advisor or such other professional advisor) before using any of the suggested remedies, techniques, or information in this book.

Upon using the contents and information contained in this book, you agree to hold harmless the Author from and against any damages, costs, and expenses, including any legal fees potentially resulting from the application of any of the information provided by this book. This disclaimer applies to any loss, damages or injury caused by the use and application, whether directly or indirectly, of any advice or information presented, whether for breach of contract, tort, negligence, personal injury, criminal intent, or under any other cause of action.

You agree to accept all risks of using the information presented inside this book.

You agree that by continuing to read this book, where appropriate and/or necessary, you shall consult a professional (including but not limited to your doctor, attorney, or financial advisor or such other advisor as needed) before using any of the suggested remedies, techniques, or information in this book. While the book refers to real-life situations, the names mentioned may have been changed.

Chapter 1: My Story

I was the crybaby of the family. None of my cousins would play with me because they said I was "too sensitive" and cried easily. Actually they were probably more afraid of incurring the wrath of my father for making his daughter cry. I don't think my father was being overly protective; more like he was vexed by a crying toddler. Even as a young child I instinctively knew my mother favored my younger sister. She was the perfect child who played quietly by herself while mummy napped. I, on the other hand, demanded a lot of attention and "discipline".

To compensate I grew up to be an overachiever in school and in sports. I excelled in everything except my own personal life. I became a "Yes-er" to everyone till I became a burnout. This self destructive pattern created a lot of inner resentments and upheavals in my relationships with family and friends. There are some friends whom I no longer speak to because by the time I reached meltdown, the friendship was beyond salvage. There was also a time I didn't speak to my mother for one year because I so sick and drained by her constant and demanding neediness.

In retrospect, a lot of it was my own doing. It all stemmed from a deep rooted desire to be accepted and liked. Why? Because my highly sensitive soul was secretly (and deadly) afraid of being rejected by others.

At rock bottom, I had isolated myself and alienated most of my oldest friends. My health also nosedived as I suffered from adrenal fatigue which meant I was always tired no matter how many hours I slept. Because I was constantly tired, I couldn't function properly or handle stress and the smallest thing would set me off. I look back now and see that it probably resulted from all the years of self-neglect.

Well, you know the saying "when you hit rock bottom, the only way is up", was pretty true for me...

A few years ago I chanced upon an article on "empaths". I realized I'm not only an empath but also an HSP (highly sensitive person). I felt so relieved someone had finally correctly diagnosed my "mysterious disease" and shone a light on my "ailments". This was the piece of revelation I needed to start on my personal journey to recovery.

In this book I will now share the tools that I used in order to help you shortcut your transformation into an empowered empath. Don't wait till you hit rock bottom; but if you're there...see you at the top.

Chapter 2: Am I An Empath?

You are a highly sensitive person with an innate ability to feel and perceive other people's emotions, energies and vibrations as your own. You can often pick up people's true motivations and intentions. However, because you often unconsciously take on other people's emotions, your life tends to be influenced or affected by their desires and moods.

Most of the time you are a peacemaker and non-violent person who finds any form of disharmony uncomfortable. Because of this you tend to bottle up your feelings till it becomes detrimental to your wellbeing, or turn into an unexpected meltdown.

You tend to exude a kind of sincerity and genuine compassion that draws others, including strangers, animals and unfortunately energy vampires too.

When you visit a place, you can easily feel and unconsciously absorb the flow of strong emotions left by others in the surroundings. Often such absorption of negative energies present in the surroundings leaves you feeling drained and exhausted. This is why some empaths find public areas such as crowded shopping malls or stadiums to be overwhelming. Even watching late night TV or social media can cause you a sleepless night.

You need a great deal of self-care as these abilities can be taxing on your emotions making you unusually tired. However, you often find it difficult to set appropriate boundaries from friends, family, people or events that might affect you.

Jane knows an acquaintance Bernice who recently lost her child after a long battle with cancer. Because Jane is an empath, she felt Bernice's deep grief and sadness even though they hardly know each other. As an empath, you will probably feel a similar sadness or grief just as described and absorb them unknowingly. To shield yourself from such draining situations, there are effective tools to help you. Later in this book you will be shown 7-highly effective tools to shield yourself in your daily life.

Chapter 3: My Gifts As An Empath

Being an empath means you have certain unique gifts that are inherent in you. Most empaths focus on their difficulties and for this reason they are not able to go far in their self-discovery to honor their gifts.

Here are some unique (but not exhaustive) gifts of empaths:

a) Empaths are natural healers and can give healing energy to others through their hands, voices or by way of playing instruments. For this reason, many empaths pursue energy healing as they believe they have an inner calling to heal themselves and others.

b) The empath's sensitive smelling allows them to enjoy food, beverages, fragrances, and essential oils with more intensity. If you work to enhance your intensity in smelling, you can even smell death or disease in a person or animal which can lead to saving lives.

c) Empaths sense potential dangers before other people as their sixth sense is more tuned in.

d) Since empaths are strong in their sensitivity, they are prone to feel deeper lows and are likewise prone to feeling greater heights than people who aren't as sensitive. Most empaths have a great enthusiasm for life and experience life and joy with greater intensity. Empaths tend to be more understanding, kind, caring, and compassionate.

e) While most people without the empathic ability feel uncomfortable being alone, empaths actually crave for a lot of time to be alone and in fact isolate themselves to de-stress and balance. Empaths need to isolate themselves to recuperate.

f) Empaths can be unusually creative in life not only in the field of arts but also in experiences, possibilities, and situations. They see things differently and think about ways that others may not be able to conceptualize. Their creativity is often mislabeled.

g) Because empaths are emotional, they can easily read and interpret emotional cues. They know what a person needs and how that person feels when that specific need is not met. They are likewise good in sensing all forms of nonverbal communication and indicators of needs, both physical and emotional. They have the strong intuitive ability even for unconscious minds and for sensing the need of those who lack the ability to speak including animals, plants, infants, and the human body.

h) Empaths are more aware of peoples' thoughts and emotions and can easily tell when someone is lying to them. They have the heightened ability to see through façade that some people set up to hide what they truly feel.

i) The heightened sensitivity of empaths is truly a gift that can be sharpened. Remember that your thoughts are linked to things and what you think is what you create. You can choose to create what you want in life.

The next time you doubt your heightened awareness or sensitivity, reframe them as your gifts. When you focus on your gifts, you can create a life that is empowering instead of draining. Honor and celebrate your unique gift as an empath.

Chapter 4: Is An Empath and Being Empathic the Same Thing?

Apples and oranges are both fruits, but they are not the same thing. Being an empath and being empathic to others are two different things.

How do you know if you are an empath or someone who is empathic towards other living beings? Here's the key difference between the two:

Being empathic needs something visible and obvious, depending mostly on external cues; like seeing the emotion of the person drawn all over his face, -physical sad appearance or hearing a life-story of hardship before you can relate to this person.

However, an empath does not need such physical cues. Empaths either consciously or subconsciously take a "feel" for the person or animal, or they feel exactly what this creature feels. They don't need more engagement to know what the person is experiencing. They have automatic access to this kind of information and can even bypass the individual's intention to seclude himself from other people's prying eyes.

With such an intuitive gift, some empaths develop to become a medium or channel. Once this gift is utilized effectively, empaths can also facilitate healing for others.

Though this gift is not limited to a certain few, some people are born with a higher level of empathic ability, but like other skills, you can enhance this through constant practice to be an on-purpose empath. It only requires you to accept your gift and trust that it will be to your advantage and not a handicap that you need to hide.

Regardless of where you are on the empathy scale, an empath is nothing short of being amazing. As an empath, you often create connections along with trust, reverence, intimacy, compassion and sense of belongingness. By doing so, you expand the capacity to hold space for one another to grow, heal, and transform.

Chapter 5: Am I Also A Highly Sensitive Person (HSP)?

If you are a Highly Sensitive Person (HSP), you are likely to identify with some of the following traits:

a) Sensitive to strong sensory input

b) High awareness of subtleties in the environment

c) Easily affected by other people's moods

d) Highly sensitive to pain

e) Can be over-stimulated by caffeine

f) Easily overwhelmed by bright lights, pungent smells or loud noises

g) Easily startled

h) Unable to focus on too many things at a time

i) Appreciate art works, scents, tastes or sounds.

So how is an HSP different from an empath? The word empath means "clairsentient" which is the **ability to clearly feel energy**. In short an HSP only feels superficial emotions but an empath can feel the energy of the emotions.

What Does It Mean?

As an empath you are only dealing with your clairsentient ability which is your ability to feel energy from others and your surroundings.

But if you are both an HSP and empath, you are dealing twofold that is the above-mentioned traits of an HSP and the clairsentient ability of an empath combined.

Most people assume HSP's and empaths are the same. It is certainly more convenient to use the increasingly socially acceptable HSP label. Some empaths too prefer to identify themselves as the less complicated HSP.

As an empath you've a gift of being exceptionally good at reading faces and body language, as well as putting yourself in other people's shoes. However, this gift can sometimes be a misunderstood intuitive ability as it functions beyond what's generally acceptable, making it strange to some. An HSP on the other hand is still within the boundary of the psychological world.

Chapter 6: Your Outlook In Life As An Empath

Tina has a hard time saying no and disappointing others. She goes to great lengths to avoid conflict and accommodate family, friends and colleagues. But putting others first always leaves Tina feeling drained, weary and resentful of herself and others. She doesn't know how to speak the truth about what she really wants without upsetting others. She feels like a victim but she doesn't realize she created this dynamic in the first place. Does this sound like you?

"Before you help others, you must put on your own oxygen mask FIRST."

You hear this from the airline flight attendant every time you fly. What do you do when there is turbulence, things flying overboard, lights flickering and smoke filling the air? You, yes YOU put on the oxygen mask FIRST before you help others. Why? Because if you don't make it your first priority, you might run out of oxygen before you can help anyone else.

As an empath, your number one task is to help yourself and take care of your own needs e.g. health, financial, contentment, peace, happiness etc. Why? Because it is difficult to help others if you are going through turbulence in your own life.

Going back to Tina - Once Tina recognized this people-pleasing pattern in herself - she learned to speak her truth by practicing. Although being honest and forthright seemed awkward at first, Tina learned to balance it with kindness while being mindful of other people's feelings. People started appreciating Tina's honesty and because she used a kind tone, they gave her a kind response and respected her own needs. Remember, when you speak your truth with kindness it will be well received.

As an empath, there are a few things happening to you energetically:

a) Energy is real and can be perceived by your heightened empath senses

b) Emotional and physical sensations are energies that can flow from one individual to you

c) Your energies, unbeknownst to you, can be entwined with other people's energies

d) When you become entangled with someone, it's not something that just gets stuck in your mind but an exchange of energies as well

e) When you are emotionally affected by someone, you are not merely empathizing superficially, but literally picking up this person's energy which is why you feel drained.

In the next chapter, we will look at how you can avoid these energy-draining situations and people known as energy vampires.

Chapter 7: Why Do I Attract Energy Vampires? (And How To Get Rid Of Them)

Energy vampires don't suck blood, have fangs or turn into bats. They are normal people who like to "feed" on the life force energy of others. The relationship that is established between these two individuals is parasitic.

Known to feed on negative attentions, these energy vampires:

a) Can cause unnecessary problems like picking a fight

b) Are deceptive

c) Are notorious guilt-trippers

d) Are masters of manipulation

e) Can flip out when least expected

g) Are prone to making threats

Amanda just ended another long one-sided emotional phone conversation with her mum. Amanda's mum is twice-divorced with a knack for creating high dramas in her life. Not a week goes by without her offloading her latest real-life dramas on Amanda. While her mum feels better after each offloading session, Amanda feels herself shrinking inside. Sometimes, she feels so drained and burdened by her mum's highly charged dramas that she has to crawl into bed and call in sick the next day.

Amanda's mum is a typical energy vampire -she is not evil and has no intentions of hurting Amanda. Like most, they are victims of their own thinking and they feel paranoid, helpless, and powerless. This is why some crave attention, strive for unattainable perfection and are preoccupied with being right. They self-medicate and engage in undesirable behaviors by creating dramas in their lives.

People like Amanda's mum are not aware that they are creating their own reality and dramas because they lack the mentality to focus on what they have done. They do not trust themselves to be able to fulfill their own needs. They don't believe that it is possible for the love they've earned -to materialize. They only believe that they could have it if they take it from others by drawing attention to themselves constantly.

But Why Do I Keep Attracting Them?

As an empath, I am constantly drawn to those in need (and vice versa). But do you know these energy vampires don't want to be healed? Their dramas are often unnecessary and self-made. The only thing they want from us, empaths, is the attention that we shower them with they come to us with the latest problem.

Energy vampires are survivalists as long as they have us as their food source. They don't have the desire to be healed or take care of themselves responsibly. The more you try to solve their problems for them, the more problems they are going to create for you. Think of their dramas as the never-ending Candy Crush game...

Energy Vampires Are Mirrors Of My Self-Worth

"My own insecurities serve as a portal for energy vampires to get into my life".

You may have some childhood or personal issues like the feeling of powerlessness or victimhood. You may be seeking constant approval or validation from others. These co-dependence issues are their tickets to ride.

You feel good when you help others and unless you do these things, you feel unloved and unwanted. You feel guilty of your good life when others are deprived of it.

You may feel unworthy of love and friendship if you don't do something in return for them. If that's so, then you may have this addiction to attract energy vampires to fill this gap.

Are you a people-pleaser or do you like to be needed by others? Being around an energy vampire can subconsciously make you feel better about yourself since they tend to be needy.

The truth is, in order to attract an energy vampire; you need to be on the same level with them. Your core beliefs and thoughts are what create your vibrations and your emotions are your indications as to what kind of vibration you are holding.

4 Tools To Get Rid Of Energy Vampires

Thankfully you don't need garlic or wooden stakes to get rid of these energy vampires. There are simpler and more civilized tools to get rid of them in your life.

1) Strengthen Your Core Daily

One of the best ways to protect your emotions from being manipulated lies within your inner core. Once daily have an undisturbed mindfulness practice of 10 to 20mins, or visualization (see Chapter 8) where you go deeper and imagine directing the energy of the universe into yourself. This will provide you with the energy to increase your vibration level to meet each day's challenges. This practice will help you restore energy and become less affected by other less desirable energy levels.

2) Don't Engage In Conversation With Them

When you engage in a conversation with an energy vampire, you are in fact sharing your energy with them. In turn they are trying to drain you out of your own energy. Some energy vampires don't consciously realize what they are doing. But some are aware of their actions and try to steal your energy to make themselves feel better. Do you notice how drained you feel after listening to your best friend's latest (and countless) breakup? Suddenly your best friend is feeling perky and ready for her next romantic adventure, while you're left high and dry. Well, you've just been "sucked" dry by an energy vampire. Remember, avoid them as much as possible (as you would a real vampire) as they have a negative impact on your limited energy level. Make up excuses and learn to cut them off short. In time, they will get the message you are not waiting around for them to offload their latest drama and move on to their next victim.

3) Practice Positive Affirmations

Practice declaring positive affirmations such as: "I am surrounded by a positive bright light!", "I am a being of light and goodness!", "Nothing dark can go near or harm me!" Declaring these affirmations (either vocally or mentally) helps create an invisible shield against energy vampires. Channel that positive energy and it will bring you brightness when others are trying to bring you down.

4) Amp Up Your Vibration

Energy vampires are threatened in the presence of people with high vibrations. The higher your vibration, the lighter you feel in your emotional, mental and physical body. You will also experience higher personal power, peace, clarity and joy. Energy vampires who have low vibrations (meaning their energy is dense, dark and heavy) can't tolerate or get near people with higher vibrations. To amp up your vibration, use mindfulness practice and visualization (Chapter 8). To ensure your vibration and positivity remain high, you can also smile at others often. A smile naturally emits a high vibration which low vibration energy vampires are bound to feel the positive effects of. When you walk down the street and smile at someone, you're also spreading your happiness to others making it a win-win for everyone.

Chapter 8: 7 Simple Strategies You Can Use In 5-Minute To Shield Yourself

Being an empath is challenging if you don't have the right strategies. Most empaths are at peace in their own home-sweet-home minding their own business. But it's a different story once they venture into the outer world. Often they get bombarded with unwanted emotions which leave them overwhelmed. An empath feeling unexplainable anxiousness might experience physical symptoms such as migraines, indigestion and panic attacks. Empaths who are defenseless are often in danger of being overwhelmed and feeling drained by others and events around them.

You don't have to be a sitting duck anymore; it is time to put on your armor and deploy some effective tools to shield yourself.

1) "NO" Is A Complete Sentence

For an empath one of the greatest tools is learning to say "No" first. Yep, you heard me right. Always say "No" first to everything. Take some time to consider if it's worthwhile and -if you change your mind later, you can change it to a "yes".

The most common challenge with empaths is we tend to say "yes" to everything, even when we really meant "no". Saying "yes" tends to be our default mode and we end up agreeing to horrible dates, imposing over-stayers, unreturned loans etc. Why? Because empaths tend to be incurable people-pleasers. We often fear being rejected or disliked so much that we stop being true to ourselves. There is a heavy price and burden to bear when we say "yes" to everything. Often it has cost me more than I dare to admit.

Saying "No" to your grandma, dad, mom, sister or colleagues does not mean you are being selfish or unkind. Remember your opinion of yourself is more important than theirs. Many people, including those closest to us, do not understand the dilemma that empaths have to battle every day. Yes, I've some free time but I'd really like to chill this weekend with a good read rather than paint your house for free. You see what I mean? There will always be one thing after another cropping up for our attention until we learn to say "No". Especially if we have family members or friends who are also energy vampires.

Helpful tips for saying "No":

a) "NO" is a complete sentence.

b) Don't delay and say "I'll think about it".

c) Don't apologize.

d) Don't lie or make up excuses for wanting some time to yourself.

e) In case you falters, recall how resentful you felt the last time you said "yes".

f) Lastly, when you speak your truth with kindness, it will be well received.

Of all the tools, learning to say "No" has been my biggest lesson as an empath. Now I feel more in control and less resentful towards others for "coercing" me into doing things. I also feel freer knowing I'm no longer dependant on others for validation.

2) Smart Recovery

Being in any kind of relationship can be draining and strenuous for an empath, especially if you tend to attract energy vampires.

Empaths need plenty of time to be alone and recharge away from family, friends and even pets. When was the last time you took some time off by yourself to reboot?

Take care of your health as your top priority by eating mindfully and healthily so that you have plenty of physical energy for the day. As much as possible, decline obligations and avoid negative triggers e.g. turn off your phone at bedtime, create personal distance or space, avoid watching bad news or horror shows on TV before bedtime.

By the way, you don't have to lay in bed all day in your PJ's. Here are some ideas to get you rebooted:

a) Get your eight hours of beauty sleep

b) Wake up earlier to practice mindfulness

c) Take up yoga or some light exercise

d) Make yourself a healthy breakfast

e) Sit in a park and enjoy the outdoors

f) Say no to something you don't want to do (without feeling guilty)

g) Say yes to something you haven't done before (tattoo?)

h) Get a massage and a facial (full works!)

i) Get a manicure, pedicure and a haircut (why not?)

j) Clean your house and de-clutter unwanted stuff by giving away to charity

k) Read a good book and doze off after 2 pages

l) Re-watch a favorite movie by yourself

m) Learn to bake or cook a new recipe

n) Sing and dance to your favorite song on radio

o) Start a gratitude journal

p) Cuddle with your kitty or play fetch with your doggy

q) Buy flowers for yourself

r) Smile, Laugh out loud ...Tell yourself in the mirror, "I love you."

Seclude yourself from the rest of the world until you feel fully recharged and ready to face the world again. And remember don't apologize for it.

3) Breath Works... Breathe In, Breathe Out

Sometimes you suspect you have absorbed someone's negative energy and need to recover quickly. You can do this quick exercise by focusing on your breath by closing your eyes. This process focuses and connects you to your higher power while keeping negative energies away. To purify your energy field, imagine you are releasing unwanted emotions when exhaling and upon inhaling draw calmness into your being. Repeat this simple exercise until you feel lighter. End by visualizing a white light entering your body and driving a dark fog away. Remember: practice makes perfect.

Anna has the perfect family of a doting husband and two children. Well, everything is perfect except for her demanding traditional Italian-only speaking mother-in-law. She did not approve of her son marrying non-Italian Anna and did nothing to hide her displeasure. Each time she visits her grandchildren, she showers them with granny love while ignoring Anna completely. Tonight, Anna slaved all day to cook a sumptuous and hopefully authentic Italian dinner for her mother-in-law. But the old lady was not pleased and even though Anna barely understood Italian, her body language and gestures told her enough.

Anna knew she was about to burst into tears and have a melt-down. She quickly excused herself and hid away in the bathroom. She needed to recover her composure quickly. She closed her eyes and told herself mentally to breathe. Inhale....and...exhale..... She felt more peaceful as she imagined a while light shrouding her and healing her. She was ready to re-join the dinner downstairs and told herself she may as well enjoy the dinner she cooked. She then started enjoying herself and even told a few jokes. At the end of the night, she bid her grumpy mother-in-law farewell without dwelling further on what happened earlier. Anna knew she will no longer be affected and held hostage by her mother-in-law's approval of her, because she now draws on her fortress of light.

4) Create Physical Distance Or Barriers

When possible, physically remove yourself from any source of negative energy e.g. a gossipy aunt or complaining colleague. Observe the instant relief after putting some distance between yourself and them. If there are some known energy vampires, don't sit next to or nearby as closeness increases your vulnerability to them.

Adam started experiencing these symptoms about a year ago after reading some resources about psychic ability and practicing meditation. Sometimes he could feel a sort of chill at the back of his neck or in the middle of his shoulder blades. His muscles would tense and his jaw would harden involuntarily. He noticed this happened every time he is in a room with an emotionally charged person or energy vampire. Nowadays he trusts his instincts and quickly moves away from the negative energy source.

5) Still Yourself With Mindfulness Practice

When we still our mind and body, we are slowing down to connect inwards with our higher self. In stillness we become more aware of our purpose and connection in life, so that we learn to flow with life. If you are facing challenges at work or have an important decision to make, use mindfulness practice to fortify yourself.

The mindfulness practice I'm showing you is very simple and only requires you to become an observer of your thoughts. Do not judge. Just sit and observe like an outsider. Start by finding a comfortable and quiet place. Sit cross-legged, lotus or half lotus on a cushion, or use a straight-back chair with your feet planted on the ground. Try to keep your spine straight. Gently close your eyes and repeat your favorite mantra e.g. "OM", or word e.g. "Peace" in your head repeatedly. Whenever you get distracted with thoughts (about a thousand times), just return to your practice. If you fall asleep or daydream, just return to your practice till time's up. If you have an incredible itch, just scratch it and return to your practice. You can start by setting your timer for 5mins and progress till 20mins. Trust in the process and allow whatever thoughts that come up to float away like a balloon without attachment. With practice, you will become more discerning and less caught up in the storylines you create in your mind.

Jerome is a new teacher in a high school located in a rough neighborhood. Most of the students come from dysfunctional families. The first time Jerome entered the class, his empath senses were overloaded with negative energies coming from his students. He didn't expect it to be so difficult and almost wanted to quit on his first day.

Jerome's lifelong dream was to help under-privileged kids. He committed to waking up earlier to do 20mins of mindfulness practice every morning to fortify his empath senses. After a few weeks, Jerome felt stronger and more in control of his unruly students. His empath sensitiveness helped him to guide some students who were acting out to get attention. Once the students sensed Jerome's resolve and dedication, they became more cooperative and open to learning.

6) The Power Of Visualization

Research has shown that visualization can heal the mind and body. It is also a well-known fact that many top athletes, for example Tiger Woods and Michael Phelps, use visualizations to improve their games. Science also shows that our brains respond more attentively to images rather than plain words.

When we visualize something, we are actually stimulating and increasing blood flow to our brain. As empaths we can use visualization as a tool by imagining a protective shield covering us from negative energies. When you have people that are extremely toxic around you, visualize a powerful sword guarding your energy field and keeping you safe from them. Pick your mental shield, it can be a powerful sword, angel, bodyguard, warrior, or ferocious tiger.

If you have difficulties with visualization, you can try carrying a powerful or inspiring picture in your wallet or cell phone e.g. majestic eagle, archangel or, mountain. Take one minute to stare at your picture and conjure the feeling of healing energies surrounding you.

Sarah was in the park sitting on one of those wooden benches reading a book by her favorite author. She was deep in her reading when she felt a dull headache. Her past experience warned her it was some energy trying to seep into her.

She felt her body tremble and her perspiration ran cold while she tried to locate the source of the intruding energy. Then she saw, seated not far away from her, a disheveled-looking man sitting depressingly with his head down and palms covering his face. Sarah didn't need to be an empath to tell the man was deeply troubled.

In this situation, Sarah was of no help to the man because she herself was acutely affected and immobile by his pain. Sarah knew she was in no condition to run to someone's rescue. Instead she quickly got up to escape into her car which was parked nearby. Once safely inside, she visualized a powerful sword shielding her from negative energies that tried to follow her. The powerful sword serves as her energy shield protecting her from the intrusion of undesirable energies.

7) Protective Stones & Crystals And Mirror

Stones and crystals carry metaphysical properties that can assist the wearers in different manners. As empaths we can utilize stones that carry protective qualities and even the ability to absorb or deflect negative energies.

Personally, I wear an obsidian bracelet daily as it offers one of the highest protection and shields me from any psychic, emotional or physical attack. I also have a small obsidian ball at my bedside to purify negative energy and aura.

Here are some protective stones and crystals for consideration:

a) Amethyst

b) Amber

c) Brown calcite

d) Charoite

e) Diamond

f) Emerald

g) Fire agate

h) Hematite

i) Yellow jasper

j) Kunzite

k) Labradorite

l) Lapis lazuli

m) Obsidian

n) Black onyx

o) Peridot

p) Smoky quartz

q) Clear quartz and rutilated quartz

r) Black sapphire

s) Tigers eye

t) Black tourmaline

u) Turquoise

Take your time when picking out your special crystal or stone. Activate your empath powers when you hold and feel the crystal in your hands. Does it feel like the right crystal for you energetically? Upon bringing it home, cleanse it first in salt water overnight.

For an emergency fix against negative energies, you can also use sea salt or table salt. Place it in a small pouch to carry along with you. The salt will help you absorb negativity but has to be replaced regularly (please discard and don't consume).

Lastly you can use a powerful feng shui method of placing mirrors strategically to redirect energy. You can carry a small mirror in your bag or place one on your work desk to repel negative energies.

When I first moved into my new home, I had a neighbor who was very nosy and complaining during the renovation works. She would often stop by at my place to snoop or scold my contractors for creating too much noise or dust. In spite of it, I really wanted us to be peaceful neighbors and not offend her. So I sent her peaceful wishes and strategically placed a small mirror inside a shoe cabinet that faced her home wall-to-wall. From that day onwards, she never bothered me again and we became civil neighbors. Win-win.

Oliver is an empath and also HSP (highly sensitive person). One of his gifts as an empath is his high creativity and vivid imagination. He loves his work as an interior designer in a well-known firm. But he dreads his critical boss and his frequent mood swings. Once he humiliated Oliver in front of the whole office over a slight mistake. Being highly sensitive Oliver felt deeply hurt by the public criticism. He had to take some anxiety pills to calm down so that he could survive the day. The next day Oliver couldn't get out of bed and had to call in sick.

A week later, Oliver's boss was in another one of his dark moods. Oliver could see from his desk that his boss' bloodshot eyes were darting around looking for his next target. He looked in Oliver's direction, but it seemed like he did not notice Oliver at all. Frustrated, he walked towards the copier machine and gave it a few kicks. Oliver knew his boss crankiness was probably due to the stress of having an autistic son at home and not personal. Oliver lightly touched the crystal pendant he was wearing underneath his shirt and thanked it for shielding him.

Practice makes perfect. Remember the first time you learned how to ride a bicycle or drive a car? Familiarize and practice shielding yourself with these seven tools till they become second nature to you.

Chapter 9: Embracing Your Gifts

An empath can sense, feel, and read energy. Learn to accept who you are and own all your abilities. Love yourself enough and don't suppress the real you. Trusting yourself and your intuitive ability is a skill to your advantage. Trust that you know how to handle this gift.

Being sensitive and having this gift is not a flaw in your character. Learn to honor your emotions because they are real. Do not be ashamed of showing how you feel even if seems ridiculous to others. These feelings won't simply go away and they need to be processed. Don't dim your light just to match someone else's light but rather crank up the dimmer switch and make them match yours. Shine bright for others and influence them with your brightness.

Bonus Guide:

1) Self Empowerment

Every time an empath sees someone dwelling in negative emotions, they always try to get that person to feel better. An empath wants to feel better around people basking in negative emotions and try to create harmony. When they run up against something unpleasant, their instinct is to take care of it. An empath loves to clean the muddy gutters and oftentimes finds themselves covered with the mud instead.

Learn to observe and not absorb! If you see people in pain, let them undergo what's for them. It will make them strong and they are entitled to experience it, so don't fix it for them. It's not yours and they need the emotion to heal them. Take charge of your emotion and let happiness be your priority. Your life is your responsibility. When these people get over their own stuff, they can be able to be in level with your emotions and not bring yours down.

Empower yourself with the good things in life so when you're up in your vibrations, no one can pinch your energy off from its source. With an ample flow of energy, no energy vampires can get in your way.

2) Self Awareness

Practice self awareness of your surroundings and people. When you are somewhere and you suddenly feel strong emotions suffocating you, remain calm. Use one of the seven tools you learned earlier to help you. Don't get overwhelmed. Remember these negative energies are not your own and you don't have to absorb them. Observe them and be on your way.

3) Forest Bathing

Forest bathing known as Shinrin-yoku in Japanese. The Japanese realized when a person visits nature it produces many health benefits such as rejuvenation, restoration and calmness. The scientific proven benefits include stronger immunity, reduced blood pressure and stress, mood enhancement, improved energy level and sleep.

The Japanese approach their forest bathing leisurely and with no efforts (meaning no step counting or hiking). The point is to be at rest with nature and let it be your tonic. You can sit underneath a tree or meander, but the whole idea is to relax. To end the walk, you can - ground your electrical field to bring back your balance by walking barefoot on the ground.

If you live in a place far from forests, you can go to the nearest park or bring nature inside your home. Buy or grow plants, do some natural landscapes, surround yourself with plants and connect with animals too.

When you take time to harmonize with Mother Nature, it will also help you develop deeper, clearer intuition and increase your vibrations.

4) Power Up With Sleep

Empaths need to have an adequate amount of rest and sleep to function more than normal people. This is because as an empath, you feel more deeply than others. Anything from unwanted emotions, stormy weather, lightning, sounds or scents can feel intense for empaths.

As part of your gifts, you naturally draw people who need help. Unwittingly you might become a confidant whom others (energy vampires) unload their baggage onto. Being a dependable person, you often serve as a lighted candle in their darkest times. But you also get burnt in the process. Because of all these daily exposures, empaths tend to be easily exhausted and drained.

A typical empath usually takes a while to unwind and unravel the assault of energies that they encounter daily. Getting ready for bed often takes hours, but it is important to untangle yourself as much as possible to have a peaceful night's sleep. Make it a ritual to practice any of the seven tools in Chapter 8 to help you prepare for sleep.

My bedtime ritual is: I place an obsidian ball by my bedside to clear away any negative aura or energies I've brought home. I'll do a 20 min mindfulness practice or -visualization to help me unwind. I also avoid watching news on TV or any disturbing shows. If I need to watch something, I'll always pick comedies.

5) Stay Healthy

Most empaths tend to forget about themselves just to accommodate the needs of other people. For instance, you forgot to take your meal in order to assist a sick friend; or you have to do overtime at work to do a favor for a colleague. It's a classic picture of self-sacrificial empaths.

Learn how to value your body as it's the seat of your life and health. If you're unhealthy, how can you live a quality life or help others? Prioritize yourself by eating nutritious food, know when to relax and rest, and if possible do some light exercises like yoga.

6) Keeping Balance In Your Relationships

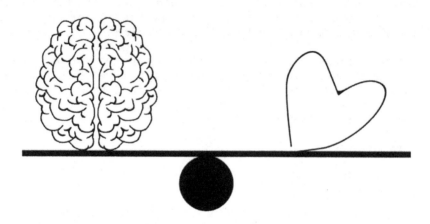

Empaths are emotional beings who experience the highs and lows of life like a roller coaster. Sometimes, you have this need for intimate physical, emotional and spiritual bonding with the people you value. Other times, you suddenly withdraw from them into your own shell. You can be intense and aloof, hot and cold all in a day.

When it comes to romance, you are usually the giver rather than the receiver. This makes you a magnet for narcissists and energy vampires. You can't always be the knight or princess in shining armor doing all the rescuing. Remember, all healthy relationships are based on give and take. You are worthy to receive love too.

Learn to be mindful and observe what's happening in all your relationships e.g. parents and child, siblings, friends, partner. Analyze and take proper measures to balance them, so that the scale is not always tipping at you as the primary giver.

Adeline's new beau Max just got a new apartment but he was clueless on how to throw a housewarming party. Adeline gladly volunteered. She happily bought and prepared everything for the party. On the night of the party, instead of playing host or helping Adeline, Max went to the party like he was a guest. Meanwhile Adeline was slaving in the kitchen, serving up food and drinks to Max's friends. Halfway through, Adeline realized she was the one who allowed these kinds of things to happen in all her past relationships. She threw down her apron, took a glass of red wine and joined the party.

Don't wait till your breaking point or when you're already burnt out before you act. Remember, you're not only doing this for yourself but also for the relationships of all the people you're involved with.

Chapter 10: Empath's Quick Guide to Living

According to research, high sensitivity affects almost 20% of the entire population. These 20% are known to be extremely sensitive and are often misunderstood by society as being "overly sensitive". Because of this, some empaths choose to withdraw from the world and shut themselves in.

You Are Uniquely Created

Empaths are uniquely created and special. Intuition is an empath's secret weapon. You can feel life's energy flow, read people and hear nature speaks. You have a big heart that opens up to those in need. You are also an idealist and a dreamer with a great thirst for life. Most empaths are also highly creative, passionate, compassionate and visionary.

On the other side of the scale, empaths can be easily over stimulated as they feel emotions ten times more than normal people. Even watching or reading bad news can affect you deeply. Some empaths also have a knack for attracting an endless pool of energy vampires. It's no wonder some empaths no longer feel inspired, creative and zesty for life with all that dead weight on them.

On the physical level, some empaths can be ultra sensitive to light, temperature, sound, smell and taste, making it hard for them to tolerate overbearing sensory input. For instance, you may be terrified or get startled easily by loud noises, thunder or even the sounds of fireworks. You might also feel dizzy or nauseous when you encounter strong scents.

Being an empath might have some inconveniences, but know that as a human being you also have the ability to adapt.

Extra Care Package For Empaths

Just like you learned tools to shield yourself in Chapter 8, there are also specific strategies and plans to take extra care of yourself. The main aim of this action plan is to help you protect your own sensitivities and bring out your full potential as an empath.

1) Types Of Empaths

Do you know there are different types of empaths? What you need to do next is to identify which type you are. Are you a physical, an emotional or an intuitive empath? If don't have an idea which one you are, here's a list to guide you:

a) Physical Empath: You are sensitive to the physical symptoms felt by people around you. Their sense of well-being can revitalize or energize you.

b) Emotional Empath: You have the ability to absorb other people's feelings and emotions. You can feel their sadness, happiness, fear or anxiety as if they were your own.

c) Intuitive Empath: You definitely have an overwhelming sense of intuition and spirituality. Depending on your forte, you can use telepathy; see and interpret visions; communicate with nature, and contact spirits.

d) Mediumship Empath: - You have the ability to contact spirits.

e) Psychic and Telepathic Empath: You have the ability to receive or absorb intuitive information.

f) Precognitive Empath: You have the ability to see visions of the future either while you're awake or dreaming.

g) Animal Empath: You have the ability to communicate with or feel the emotions of animals.

h) Plant Empath: You have the ability to connect and feel the needs of plants.

i) Earth Empath: You have the ability to assimilate the weather, the Earth as well as the Solar System.

I'm sure by now you already have an inkling of your "super powers" and might want to consider developing it further.

2) You Are Not Mother Theresa

This is a gentle reminder that being compassionate doesn't mean you have to say "Yes" all the time. Learn to say "No" first (see Chapter 8). How can you help others when you are already depleted? Accept the fact that others are also capable of overcoming their own obstacles and life challenges without your interference or assistance.

3) Let Yourself Loose

Empaths are naturally born creative; all you need to do is let yourself be. Find an outlet to express yourself e.g. writing, painting, singing, acting, designing etc. Release what you have bottled up inside and express yourself authentically.

4) Be Your Own Best Friend

Be your own best friend and advocate. Don't neglect the need to tend to yourself. It's especially easy to forget in today's fast paced life with technology and social media bombarding us round the clock.

Take time to reboot regularly. Eat healthily, drink lots of water and get adequate sleep. Mediate or take a walk in nature. Spend quiet time with a book. Regularly do things that revitalize you. When you take care of yourself, you are offering the best version of you to the universe.

Epilogue

Being an empath is like being in alcoholics anonymous. We will always be somewhat vulnerable. Some days I still struggle with the guilt of saying "no", especially to family. I am still prone to fatigue when I'm stressed out and my adrenal is firing up. But I keep trying even if it's baby steps, because I know change won't happen until we start seeing and doing things a new way.

This book is not about me, it's about YOU. You were not given a choice to be an empath but you do have a choice to decide if you want to change. You really have nothing to lose, so pick one or two of your favorite strategies from Chapter 8 to begin.

It's my deepest desire that this book has helped you embrace your unique empath gifts and unlock your superpowers. Be an empowered empath and shine your light for the world.

Sending you love and light,

-- Sandy Quinn

P.S. I'll be most grateful if you can kindly leave a supportive review on Amazon and share what you liked. Together we can spread the word to help others. Thank you so much!

https://www.amazon.com/dp/B07191ZKZD

Check Out My Other Book

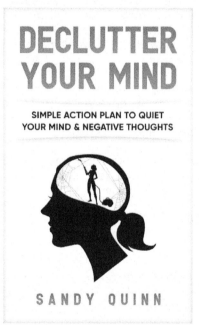

Declutter Your Mind: Simple Action Plan To Quiet Your Mind & Negative Thoughts
(https://www.amazon.com/dp/B071Z55WR9)